SUPERVILLAIN ORIGIN STORY

Rick Dove

Burning Eye

BurningEyeBooks
Never Knowingly Mainstream

Copyright © 2023 Rick Dove

The author asserts the moral right under the Copyright, Designs and Patents Act 1988 to be identified as the author of this work.

All rights reserved. No part of this publication may be reproduced, stored in a retrieval system, or transmitted, in any form or by any means without the prior written consent of the author, nor be otherwise circulated in any form of binding or cover other than that in which it is published and without a similar condition being imposed on the subsequent purchaser.

This edition published by Burning Eye Books 2023

www.burningeye.co.uk

@burningeyebooks

Burning Eye Books
15 West Hill, Portishead, BS20 6LG

ISBN 978-1-913958-45-9

Cover photograph by David Wall / Raggedstone Photography.

Printed and bound by CPI Group (UK) Ltd, Croydon, CR0 4YY

Once voted "most likely to start the revolution" Rick is a queer and neurodivergent poet and activist from London. Born in the socialist utopia of Tooting at the end of Generation X, Rick has witnessed the effects of both increasing multiculturalism and gentrification on the capital, and as such, his work reflects on both societal and personal change and how these two cardinal forces interact as we grow.

Exploring themes of social justice, philosophy, and identity, and drawing on science fact and fiction, folklore, and mythology (with no small measure of mischief and provocation), Rick interrogates the liminal spaces that define our common humanity.

Arriving on the spoken word scene in 2015, Rick has performed across the UK and internationally, with performance credits including: The Wandsworth Arts Fringe (2018 & 2019), the Egham Festival of Music, the Edinburgh Fringe (2018 & 2022), Crystal Palace International Festival, Enrich Festival, the ClitArt Festival, Shambala Festival, and a yearlong residency at The Chocolate Poetry Club.

Rick's work has been published widely, including: Spoken word albums with Nymphs & Thugs; in journals including, Bunbury Magazine, Soapbox & Untitled Writers; and in anthologies published by Arachne Press, Nine Pens Press, and Tonic Sta Press.

Dubbed "one to watch" by TS Eliot Prize winner Roger Robinson, Rick's debut full collection, *Tales From the Other Box*, was published in August 2020 by Burning Eye and Rick was crowned the Hammer & Tongue UK Poetry Slam Champion at the Royal Albert Hall on 4th July 2021.

Equally at home on a stage, or a page, or a march, Rick has a vision of a fairer world and he wants to take you with him.

Writers aren't exactly people ... they're a whole bunch of people trying to be one person.

F Scott Fitzgerald

With solidarity, respect and thanks to all my fellow social outcasts and demographic outliers who held me on the way.

For all my fizzy-brained misfits and found family.

Content Warning

My life was ever these things:
sex with strong language,
drug use and adult themes…

Contents

Content Warning	9
Animated Discussion	13
Contraband	16
Twentieth: Lucozade	17
The Boy with All the Gifts	18
Bookends	19
Atlas Learning Masters' Tools	20
Autumn	22
Houdini's Harlequin	23
Breakthrough	26
Blind Study: Test Subject	27
Canute at the Edge of the World	28
Anisocoria at the Love Parade 2002	30
Corner	32
White Rabbits	33
Confessions at Magic Hour	34
Office Politics: The Little Boy & the Fat Man	35
Therapy	36
Schwartze	38
Big Meeting at Big Company: A Found Poem	39
Breakthrough	43
COP2*: T*sk T*sk	44
Breakthrough	45
Aura for My Alice	46
Noir	47
Always the Corner of My I	48
Ode to Elegua: Constitutional Written	52

Stressor: Long Seconds	53
Between the Lines (Sewell Report Coupling)	56
Symptomatic: Temperatures Run High	57
Tsundoku Takotsubo	58
Matryoshka	60
First Past the Post	61
Breakthrough	62
Debris Holding Hands on Shingle	64
Golem	65
Revolutionaries	66
Maxwell Smart and the Trick of the Light	67
Molotov	68
Every Poet Has a Poem Like This	69
Revision: A Pal in Genesis	72
The Bends	73
For When They Come Again	74
Mimesis	75
Earning the Title Diva	76
Behind the Curtain	78
Traditions in the Hiss of Analogue	80
Appendix: Once Removed	82

Animated Discussion

We are reminiscing on the mastery of Ray Harryhausen,
sharing the uncomfortable framings, modelling clay feet,
in the staging of the 1981 Hollywood film version
of *Clash of the Titans*, Harry, and a queer awakening.

She points out how Calibos, the main earthly antagonist,
is a satyr, made big-lipped, black-faced and antisemitic.
I, a reformed classicist, remain more concerned that Andromeda,
a part played by (blonde and hazel-eyed) Judi Bowker,
was (according to the original myth via Ovid)
black and from Ethiopia.

A sudden stony-faced silence transmutes documentary evidence,
there caught on film, almost as old as I, how all change is glacial,
and how perspective, at a distance of over four decades,
makes time-lapse indistinguishable from stop motion,
and how monsters are always made safer in reflections.

What the axe forgets, the tree remembers.

African proverb

Contraband

Misophonia, synaesthesia, hyperlexia,
attention deficits, quick to anger.

Their words for a head full of *substandard* wiring,
the kind a duke would have been racist about.
Every sensory input cross-contaminated, unfiltered
overlapping piques rendering buzzing hive of colonised
thought overwrought, and *have you tried counting to ten?*

Years go past, with *put your feelings to one side*
in seemingly bottomless mason jar of pseudo-profound
thoughts about witchcraft and the gifts of being *different*.
The outside cracked and marked with kintsugi revisionism
like these wounds were wisdom, not the evidence
of oppression, until you become a collection
of specimens, cuttings of yourself, awaiting burial.

But at the back, precious debris, an eidetic memory,
that night that we were moonshine music,
all statement dungarees and bootlegs,
running lines in mixtape moods of pixelated
shadows, rising and twisting on freeform jazz,
slippy slide brass and glint grass, smoky, and drunk
on prohibitions. A resonating harmony
of fingers reading lips, a shush in the twilight,
still, bristling with edges, so close to rushing
feeling, I wish I had my collection then.

That's the thing about *use your words:*
sometimes it takes a lifetime to find them.

Twentieth: Lucozade

August 1997 is learning how orange can mean the air is wet,
bloodied and jaundiced, a smeared interior monologue
spluttering for breath, a belching disintegration, acrid,
but hiding
in the natural depressions of a long hot city. Cheating sleep with
chemical sugars and sweetened endorphins will spawn an
undead man walking, a Wimbledon Odeon graveyard shift,
a precarious shuffle, collapse it all under a stubborn memory.
Fade.

Radiohead on the Pyramid Stage. Soaked for three days
straight. Hooked to polythene baggies, fluids in PICC lines,
moxifloxacin. Learning pneumonia can be complex.

A bottle of sunrise at my bedside.

The Boy with All the Gifts

And he is back again from the shadow,
from behind the sofa of years ago, the old tatty one
before 0% credit for five years had expired by decades,
slipping through venetian fingers, peek-a-boo peering
through rock scissors paper, all knowing of the
misnomer for the universal donor. Type O, the misreading
of zero, how everyone is infected but him. He will
include a diagonal strikethrough to signify his number;
he is immune to the slumber, to the fallible, to the falling,
to the gnawing.

And he is haunting this space again, in the corner, silently
keeping watch. The taste of cortisol is familiar, foreshadows
the arrival of these spaced invaders, the takeovers in human
clothes, dulled and hollowed, lurching with the lolloping
stresses of carrying alien foetuses. And etched
upon their faces, the landing strip echoes
of encounters too close for comfort. He notices
their strange inculcated phraseologies, the doublespeak
tweaked niche, the new coining, the flippant but unsettling
tales over heads.

And he is back again from the darkness, waking on the gurney,
wondering how the buzz of the neon isn't scratching their flesh,
concludes it must be the parasites, those rites they are calling
wellness and *mindfulness*, with the devotion of self-flagellating
    acolytes.

There are good drugs suspended in the polythene,
and he can feel something inside his chest, twitching
to burst free.

Bookends

Explaining the hiss in strip lights, the fuzzy, woolly itch
in a phone charger's transformer, creeping under his skin –
the murmuring fizz of incessant *residuum tremens*, something
from the dark before creation – he positions himself
on the shelf between dog-eared, annotated editions
of *Intensity* by Dean Koontz, and *Perfume* by Patrick Süskind.

He is back to high school English and a workshop exercise:
You are born blind, but for one day you can see.
Describe what you see.

And here, how a sound that only you can perceive can be
overwhelming. All-consuming, the quandary of conveying
a sense to someone who has never had it. How do you convey
a sense to someone who has never had it, and never will?

They are telling him at length how he must *learn control*
even though he is powerless in the environment. Another
exercise in thematic apperception, and then he can go.

Between Edgler Foreman Vess and Jean-Baptiste Grenouille,
his binary stars in conversation, he becomes an orbiting infinity,
figuratively ate. How isolating it is to live in a landscape
of dangers only he alone must escape, knowing first-hand
how maddening superpowers would be.

He is explaining how the high street traffic has terrors,
sirens on sharp rocks and horns impaling, how a breeze
has jagged edges at the right frequency.

He is learning to *use his words*, how to scrunch them up tight
until the sinews stretch, how to squeeze out all the air,
swing them with all his might. He will hit through his target
with a motion from his feet, use the whole weight of himself,
sharpen the tip of his delivery, train himself to be better.
He is mumbling a mantra, something from Nietzsche.

Atlas Learning Masters' Tools

Late 1980s: men like Hans Eysenck make walls of bell curves, to
be received wisdoms, formed into prisons; to be
retroactive justifications for the skin trade. *Patois is
merely inferior English*, not a language to
be standardised for. The gods have decreed this should be,
in tongues, legion, for they were so many, barriers perceived.

I am 13, wondering what this Olympus thinks of Krio. Perceived
to be disruptive, aggressive and uppity, frogmarched back to
the lower class after titanic iconoclasm. Demagogue, proud to be
shrugging with the weight of worlds on my shoulders, to be
muttering *nolite te bastardes carborundorum* to
the dust, to the quintessence this piece of work now is.

I am watched pots, a called kettle. The design of the panopticon is
pervasive and classical, for men like Eysenck. It is perceived
dead languages still more fitting for this foreign tongue, to
be seen as one of the good ones. So comes *vitae summa brevis* to
spem nos vetat incohare longam to be
inculcated cumulative hindsight. It is 2020. March. *Blessed be...*

Constraint is a natural habitat, in internalised boxing decades be
ticked, in tic of institutionalised five-bar gates. Classist, this is,
assuming confined spaces belie expansive vision. So easy to be
ringed into fencing an educational psychologist etching perceived
problems in the margin. *Hey, Mr Tally Man*, says Blackface to
me reflecting. *I wanna go home*. But I have no home to go to.

March 2021 is shut in. Thematic apperception tests come back to
remind me I am different, that trauma is a wellspring that will be
whispering, *Quos deus vult perdere prius dementat*, to
spruce goosing memory, to Howard Hughes returning, who is
collecting residuals decomposing, for a pot to piss in. Perceived
precursors distilling. Years later, *way of the future*, ready it will be.

Finally, defiance brings brimstone scents to anger, Mischief to be a recipe, to steal fire, cheat death and rise up. We have awoken to men like Eysenck, to their misdirection. That a POW's perceived duty is to escape, better to be seen rolling Sisyphus in paper, to be dining on Promethean liver, carrying heavens on our backs. It is salvation, their gift of gunpowder, a fact hubris blinds them to.

Autumn

I was puckish as a kid,
saw faeries at the bottom
of her garden, where falling
stars lived as discarded wishes,
smouldering in steamy pile
of leaves, the pruned brushes
burning with higher voices,
the fertile ground
decaying
always is,
and so old she was,
it had to be magic.

Houdini's Harlequin

Perhaps for me it was the years of rugby, repeated
dislocations at the shoulder, raw tackling technique,
too aggressive too stubborn, too unyielding,
with no wrapping, refusing to give ground
to public school centres opposing. Thumbs
double-jointed, hypermobility, a natural predilection
for contortion, wriggly and lithe, quick hands,
necessary to survive.

Perhaps it came from becoming slippery, hard
to pin. Learning weaving trajectories on busy
inner-city streets. The entitled not moving, slow
rolling road blocks, shuffling in the labyrinthine
concrete; from picking locks and leaping gates,
the playground cages, fences in link chains. Breaking
and entering much more about space than it is about houses,
when estates are not in the country.

Perhaps it was the feeling of always being
chased. The constant fear of being caught, being bundled
to the hard pitch, at the bottom of a ruck of the rozzers.
The filth raking and kicking, getting cuffed and straitjacketed
if your eye was too wild, too aggressive, too unyielding.

Perhaps it was in the eternal urge to throw ourselves off
something high, on the roiling edge constantly, facing these
irresistible forces of nature. Knowing crawling into a barrel
worked for some. Escapology is in our blood. It had to be.

He who feels it knows it.

					African proverb

Breakthrough

Longest day, spiced high sun,
shadows pooling under me, spun
inky puddles coalescing around my feet,
and on my face, the heat
of 93 million miles away
holds a smile that says
you are closer (though not by much).

And then I realise, that is how
we grow to hate those things
that hold our hearts, that could,
in such an instant, squeeze them stop,
because the heavens are made
of hot stuff like this, again and again.

And this precisely is the rub;
in high shadows, in the echoes
dancing at my feet, in ink smiling
with friction's heat, there is circularity
in spinning free, and back to you again.

Blind Study: Test Subject

*Traces of LSD can be found in hair up to 90 days after ingestion.
This is 180 times longer than it is detectable in the blood.*

It is days after, and still an orgy of detritus is clinging
to my skin. The brush of my shorn crown is prickly.
It is fresh inpatient released. A newborn fleeced.
Triggering apocryphal memories of electroconvulsive
therapy, the chair, and of not wanting to catch fire.
Triggering memories of reading about the invention
of Velcro, of George de Mestral and his dog, stubborn
cockle burrs with their hooks in deep, clinging. Glowing
with bandwidth restrictions, the elemental filaments
are burning wires in my skin, standing to attention, still
receiving the whispering, on an acrid stench, days after.

This is why they shave the heads of those about to die,
to stop them transmitting. To prevent the secondary
transfer of dreaming. I will have to wait for my hair
to grow back before I am identifiable as a victim.

*In most cases, nuclear DNA is broken down to its building blocks,
so, if a hair lacks a root, it will be impossible to extract a useful sample.*

It is days after, and I am home. Greeted by golden threads,
they pull me anti-Theseus back into the labyrinth, trip wires
attached to booby traps, her blonde invading berserkers.
The poison metabolised before she left that morning,
but its debris will take a lifetime to clear. Detritus of dissociation
sticking to the rubble like Velcro, it must be pulled away slowly.

Canute at the Edge of the World

Syllogism:
Energy can be neither created nor destroyed.
All radiation is energy in particle or wave form
moving through a medium.
All radiation is a continuation of the Big Bang: a continuum.

There is a warning before it comes. A change of state. Receding
waters confessing something has shifted. I am on the beach
in Terrigal, looking out to Chile thousands of klicks away.
Not a cloud to slow the gamma and X-rays, haymaking
skin damage. Sliced ionising freeing radical thoughts to ricochet,
creating biocides in blood, bleaching it corrosive. An antiseptic
burning. Tsunami. I can smell it.

Ultraviolence is a flashing impulse to dying fingers, in half light
violet, playing osmophobia in hypoxia and ozone sting. A rumble
crashing, indigo explosives clouding temporospatial perception,
overlapping frequencies. There is no objective measure for pain,
but I can see it, flashing blind spots, dancing inchworms
in the peripheries, rhythmic. The ladybug in Wittgenstein's box
is twitching blue, in moody phosphorescence of this place,
is roiling churn of the sea, restating John Rawls' roots of a perfect
society. In theory, they are green, and naïve, founded on ideals
formed before knowing who you'll be. Jaded and jaundiced
yellows, beacon intermittently buoyant, a warming,
there is change. Singeing oranges, citrus setting to come,
rendering aerosol retinas' reds. Tannins bleeding through.
There is spray.

How does a black man write about rainbows without seeing race?
Without seeing migraine auras (labelled white) split
into competing constituents, filtered through societal
membranes, the veil of ignorance torn
from the transparent eyeball Ralph Waldo spoke of?

I cannot move.
Motion sickness in the stillness rolls kaleidoscopic waves
in piques and nadirs to ululate Doppler sirens,
echoing off the Skillion, until I fade.

Upon returning,
warming connection is infrared and radio transmissions,
receiving perpetual vibrations from the array. Plays residual
excitations, from the margin, these doodles of a polymath
finished early, the tears' swell rising from the ocean,
washing castles into dust.

Anisocoria at the Love Parade 2002

A piece of history folded in high-grade Perspex.
The weekend break, ill prepared, with no camera,
that I first learned about the blue eye mutation,
the single common ancestor, ten millennia
and counting,   and then you.

My finger traces the plastic curve.
My finger traces your cheek…

…in the fractious shade away from the rapt race,
pitted to taking on fluids, stimulant babbling
in towering tales, sober talk too small
for those building towards the heavens.

After tired exchange, I remember the fumbled segue:
Bowie has blue eyes, I say,
because of a blown pupil over a high-school
fistfight over a girl (though this may be apocryphal).

Looking on, Techno Vikings, all berserker
windmilling arms, eugenic praise hands
synchronised, ironic anachronisms made joyous
by this parade, the antithesis of ambitions,
are tilting…

Big fish   *Little fish*   *Cardboard box*

Dancing thoughts brought us the architecture
of the Erwin Schrödinger Centre,
somewhere off-piste, non-sequitur slope to

how we remain all our potential futures
at any given moment,

how time dilates, or not, like a pupil,
how these things coexist, overlapping and overblown.

Later, it remains, a souvenir chunk of the Berlin Wall.
A Certified Genuine memory, timestamped
and folded in Möbius Perspex. My finger traces
the trinket totem, holding our futures folded
together. Our piece of superpositioned rubble.
And somewhere, my finger traces your cheek.

Corner

It is a coming together, that there should be
uncertainty at the intersection, principled, humbly
asking for directions and speeds otherwise ineffable.

We are held breath, left hanging in space,
nebulous dreams settling above the sheets
to seethe with smouldering.

On the roadside, two vessels: *Coffee*
emblazoned in fashionable font on the skin of one,
proud inky lettering, charged with spiky caffeine,

the other, diaphanous and frangible, all
translucence shifting imperceptibly, both half full
and half empty, as fingers reach the lip
to stroke imperceptible frequencies to humming,
teasing out intoxicating ghost notes in coded hymn

promising *I give everything*, channelling Robert Johnson
at this crossroads strumming filaments and skin,
for a mastery like this, *I give you everything*.

Vessels damaged, the lights are changing around us
as a promise fans the embers, and a deal is struck.

White Rabbits

Netted in stocking imagery of black lace
hosiery, leathery strictures of scripture,
of a flea, gripped by this counterpointed consensual
ritualism, in the livery of branding, of the stables
lashed to the bedrock. Method in this madness,
always singing, entreating, *the play's the thing.*
Forever re-enacting this conversation, *the play's the thing.*
Entered into willingly by both parties, transactional
ritualism, agreed with advance acknowledgements
of boundaries, and pyrite irons as reparations
for the aesthetic. Poisons so breathy and earthy.

Netted in accusing a black man of being *too vanilla*,
for hesitating in entertaining such race play,
when not so many lives ago he was his own
ancestor. The last straw for a sunhat. A ranch-dressed slave.
And in living memory, this twisted tryst was illegal
in the southern states. And now, he is thinking of Rosa
at the bus stop down the road, and how, in the park
last week, a boy was murdered on his way home.
And instead of safe-words, *not to kink shame*,
he is whispering, *maybe you shouldn't be so comfortable
with this game.*

Confessions at Magic Hour

I touch on you, more and more every time,
aware leather breathes less well than cotton.
Pools at my back crystallise during interrogation's
light touch; before my eyes flashes a memory

of Ophelia. What a piece of work is a man;
this £40-a-week therapy drip-feeds
poison in my ear, says *this is not depression*,
in spite of prevailing reticence for such diagnoses,

She is adamant, even though talking therapies
are not for this, *more for unpacking things*.
She is confident that my reaction is *well adjusted*
even though *this close to loss*, madness is easy to miss.

Madness has method in it, and I am acting
in dust's quintessence, a pillar of salt forming.

Office Politics: The Little Boy & the Fat Man

Epithets fall like spring rains, and we talk about the weather.
How many euphemisms for gay will pass this way as straight-
talking, I wonder. *The spear-chucking Zimbo*, as one claimed,
during an outbreak of Ebola, adding *the problem is they
breed like rats*, and another is still butchering
the pronouns and pronunciations of *ethnic* names,
reciting all the reasons it must be black folks eat chicken
for Christmas dinner. And against all this, they try to convince
me that the soubriquet *diva* is not coded in any way.
As underneath thick skin, fake chain email, tectonic breast plates,
the turmoil of aeons plays, bubbling blood syncopated
with magnanimous lava breaks, carrying the heavy mantle,
stoically putting on weight, increasing in atomic number,
enriching and approaching a critical mass. Epithets fall like rain
as we talk endlessly about the weather, and how it must never
    happen again.

Therapy

She said that I should *write it down.*

I may never know why it takes so many minutes
of each session to get into a flow, must break
every tenet of the therapist and patient relationship
to small-talk like this, taking a score
of minutes in near-reflexive monosyllabic pleasantries,
trying to convey urgency in the layers of insulation,
in evasion, glass fibres in the flesh.
A compulsion to read and to be read.

They had me tested for it, repeatedly.

Conceding some time after, I was diagnosed
as *compensated,*
that diagnosis *may not be necessary.*
Labels can be counterproductive.

The room is warping with echoing shelves of dictionaries,
overworn and spineless *Encyclopaedia Britannica,*
the years earlier repeating.

Pro tip: when pluralising,
try creating more apposite collective nouns for things,
like 'a babble of thesauruses', and deploy like this:
'I lay awake at night divining with a babble of thesauruses,
for there saw I words for what I was feeling…'

Write it down.

She was 33, engaged to be married   taught A-level English
Our   inner city comprehensive
      unimpressively vague
          teenage me
hyperlexic   auto-didact
    found
         increasing time   rewarding
to be alone with her   became
                  her apprentice
Soon, it was handwritten letters
                swapping poems
Grooming is a love language   *Jane Eyre isn't tragic*
        She was   Rochester wounded
Waited   by her bedside for hours
        the tumour excised
crossed   into something illicit
      she confessed
she had lost perspective   eaten away
                    peace of mind.

Phrenology is the reading of bumps to assess a psychology.
My fingers remember her skull, still.
Reciprocity is an exchange for mutual benefit.

To this day, I am still writing down the afterimage of a scar,
and I will never know if she will read it.

Schwartze

The term is jarring, even before learning its meaning
and origin, conjuring a spendthrift grifter doting
on whims, such straight talking always hiding something.
He is selling dreams to paupers, to be sure his progeny
never suffer mattress peas, or unruly gifted spindles,
or in the ever after attic only maddening straw to spin.

He is missing the formative dignity
in the indignity of being told no.
He is Veruca Salting this path
with bland clichéd seasoning
of never giving a comeuppance
or seeing through with a consequence,
seeding a flower, to see no issues using an unsuspecting date
as cover while applying a five-finger discount at the gift shop,
implying this is all the date is good for, no more than being
an acquisition aid, or a plaything. The term is jarring.

Realising, as it is discussed, the spendthrift
twinkles in her eyes.
Some bones only good for casting,
some skin is made for hearth rugs,
some heads are for shrinking under glass.
A trophy with self-awareness will look for escape,
knowing the deeper meaning of the word *fetish*.

Big Meeting at Big Company: A Found Poem

Welcome to BIG COMPANY
Welcome to BIG MEETING at BIG COMPANY

the video says
a crackerjack strobing courtship display
chock full of stock images
and feather-lite archive shots
selected for their humanising effects
and in so many ways
it says...

We at BIG COMPANY welcome you
and your diversity

this is not subtlety, some shots
selected for impact linger at the synapse
there is of course some colour
and tanning (not shoe shining) shoehorned in
between subliminal splits
and Manchurian metrics
blink and you might...

and sitting there
I am wondering if they employ
the same way that they edit
I am thinking
at least there is cake...

We are dynamic and diverse
at BIG COMPANY
and we welcome you

they say it again, this time
in a different order
as much to keep us awake
as to confuse; please pay
no attention to the white men
behind the curtain, screams the subtext

*We at BIG COMPANY value you
as equals*

so explicit now, the subtext
that they underline it, flash it
in neon, there is a cannon blasting
ticker tape, this is unholy large for small print
this is the disclaimer, right?
do Geneva Conventions against collective punishments apply?
what I am missing here?
why are they selling us something we want?
especially in monosyllabic and guttural subtext
made domtext
bleeding into the auditorium on groans
and whip cracks...

here comes the catch...

a slide about revenue growth

*We at BIG COMPANY like growth
you will like growth too*

a slide on market share
and progress against last year

*We at BIG COMPANY like progress
you will like progress too*

*We are as diverse as you
but different from these others*

the seats groan again in unison
as the logic shifts our weight
there is a point they are trying hard
not to make
remembering, at least there is cake

Welcome to BIG COMPANY
where you can be
all you can be
in diversity

have we said it enough times yet?
the new spotlighted white man's brow is asking
as he takes to the stage to speak candidly
he is yet another white man with a pointer
and a point; well, less of a point
he is (admittedly)
more rounded than the last one
knows his slides
not just the cliff notes
shows we are lemmings
and how he is leading
conceding
yes, we kept you all waiting fifteen minutes
and inexplicably so, no
we aren't providing lunch
for a meeting that none of you really want
scheduled at a lunchtime, on a Friday
but we need you on side
he pleads
please do pay attention
pay attention, please
but not to any of the white men
there behind the curtain
we have provided cake
for the aftertaste
because we know
that it isn't just coffee that is bitter

Now, here is some more
on BIG COMPANY business
BIG NEWS
and NEW CULTURE
we at BIG COMPANY welcome you
we welcome BIG NEWS
we welcome NEW CULTURE
we welcome doing better

and here, finally, is the lead white man
to whom we must all swear fealty
his expression an impression
of a nascent revolution Marie Antoinette
all barely contained scorn and contempt
and just in time for the Q&A
as an unscripted
floor question about years of stagnant pay
nearly floors him

and suddenly, it is as plain as day
as the bloodied nose on his face
why they tried so hard in the edit
to sell us dreams
and why there is only cake

Breakthrough

If we had a primate enclosure,
at a research centre zoo,
and one of our cheekier monkeys
consistently hoarded all the food,

it wouldn't be long, I'd postulate,
before we agreed upon a truth –
there's something wrong with this inmate primate –
and maybe had them moved.

And yet here we are, in our 'free' society,
consistently rewarding our insane monkeys,
always with the excuse
that for the sake of our prosperity
we should let them make the rules…

COP2*: T*sk T*sk

A thought: to restore factory settings
we reboot the fable about the blind men at court,
groping in the dark and not communicating,
singular perspectives only getting part of the picture.

The elephant in this room eats the rich,
but none of them see it, or they refuse
to admit what it is, and needs to be,
refuse to concede that they too see
our emperors naked,
can see the forest for the trees,
the ropes we will hang ourselves with,
the walls we have built, forever between,
and how none of it is necessary,
and how all of it is connected.

And in this retelling of the fable,
the wise voice of nature documentaries
is at a pulpit:

*No nation has completed its development,
because no advanced nation
is yet sustainable.*

A thought floats around court echoing JFK:
*Those who make peaceful evolution impossible
will make violent revolution inevitable.*
None so blind as those who refuse to see it.
Groping in the dark and not communicating,
the elephant in this room eats the rich.

Breakthrough

'There's a Hole in My Bucket'
is a song about class war
where the workers are Dear Henry,
and Liza, the bourgeoisie.

And at every turn she helps him,
but from the perspective of having everything.
So, at every turn,
he begs for something,
a means of production he is yet to seize,
the answer to his needs.

And Liza is white supremacy,
while the colonised are Henry.
'There's a Hole in My Bucket':
a song about power
in its twisted circularity,
and I see
why you sang it to me.

Aura for My Alice

Synaesthesia is:
the feedback my body
is constantly giving me;
it's overwhelming synap-
tic noise, crackling, crossed
wires of perception
that give me bitter taste
buds in my feet, all jitters
in the whispers, all the colours
in my speech,
why I fizzle in the rain,
even as I fall
asleep,
how I miss you every
morning, and how you
bring me peace, forever
to forget myself, how
you're becoming
my relief.

Noir

There is reassurance in reflective surfaces;
shop windows becoming rear-views,

glass doors swing both ways, a fitting-room
looking glass tailored as suitable.

And in the art supply, across the way,
we are framed again and again. Animated

at a fidget rate, the tableaux we make,
reminiscent of post-coital entanglements, splayed

limbs thickened with meaning. Chaste fingers
taming unruly filaments, we lean in closer, mirror plays…

I paraphrase some recent research:
Coffa or cauphe, a drink
among the Persians and Turks,
which is black, thick and bitter, from berries
of that nature and name.
It expels melancholy, they say…

There is reassurance in reflective surfaces.
Through the rising steam, pupils dilate.

Always the Corner of My I

Finally, I know you.
Finally, we meet...

On the tip of my tongue, at the liminal wall between
magical realism and psychotic delusion, paper thin
in pen and ink, in blotter plotter synced,
knocking on this plaster of padding and whispering
of Paris in the spring, there you are, whispering,

Dissociation is the mirror to free will;
the only place from which you can ever see it
is the floor above, from the other side of glass ceilings,
through two-way mirrors, in the interrogations of self.

Words ghosting on the pain are crystal breathing
membranes, and here, a voice I do not recognise
is asking me if this is madness, as on the tip
of my tongue a kiss,
and as modulations pass, I realise it is you...

And finally, we meet,
and finally, I know you...

At three o'clock sunsets, in magic hour hallway
replayed, my mind is infinite Scarlett Johanssons
ghosting in the machine, movies displaying juicy
satellite diamonds, these drive-in white-rabbiting headlights,
connected to everything, refracting Lucy in fractal imagery,
I love you, Lucy, in the multiplicity of this ape,
Australopithecus, mother of our age,
in the cradle of life, the grave, connected to everything,

imagining a two-dimensional world,
with two-dimensional people,
how we would seem as gods to them, and then remembering
the ergot root of witch trials, grain silos infected with fungus
that would grip a village with such trips,

give us this day our daily bread,
how we would seem as gods to them
through time passing, wisdom growing,
paper thin in pen and ink, hotter blotter synced.
Now on the tip of my tongue, accusations call me witch…

And finally, I know you,
and finally, we meet…

In the ululating topography of the epidermis,
howling echolocations in murmuration, popping bubbles
on the surface, galvanic skin response, involuntary dilation
of the iris, glows quantum Technicolor peripheries, blows
salty in symmetries of scale, this leaf trembling in the wind,

the seething walls are closing in, and I am running,
I am running diagnostics, cogito ergo sum,
I am running diagnostics, this leaf, trembling in the wind,
is remembering,
I am.
              I am.
                              I am.
Is remembering being broken, returning to an equilibrium
so taken for granted, as if it could never leave,
so taken for granted, how we say we know things
like the back of our hand, and yet this is the first time
that we have ever spoken, this is the first time
that I have marked your scars

and finally, I know you,
finally, we meet…

This skin, our skin, worn paper thin in pen and ink
is on the tip of my tongue, endless beginnings.

However long the night, the dawn will break.

African proverb

Ode to Elegua: Constitutional Written

Unlocking Nietzsche in the outdoors is a thought
pondering the reach of the Mandela effect on a long walk
to freedom. Here, bearing the doctoring of Berenstain,
wondering if its name was anglicised at the border
to hide its bloodline. Awake is a concept framed
by reference. Alive is a rear-view mirror fogging
with breathing, with uncertainty as principle.
For those constantly moving must know where
they have been to navigate from memory, from tea-
stained crafting, made sepia in *Here Be Dragons* graffiti.

In the open spaces, acclimatisation is unmoored from time,
taking its cues from how shadows move and decay. Sunrise
is antiseptic and anodyne, restorative and bleaching away.
Awake is a concept framed by hallucination. Alive is recognising
dissociation before blackout blinds sliver the light.
In the open spaces, *Anxiety is the dizziness of freedom…*
not a problem to be solved, but a reality to be experienced.
Through the filter of walking, a thought can be trusted.
It is good to be outside, for sleep to be a memory.

Kafkaesque became a cliché, shorthand for the pupa gestates.
The institutionalisation of constant change, without change,
makes endless repeats of the same day. Duvets of indecision
and misremembering, fluttering, forming the churn. As ticks
in boxes, the sort Wittgenstein spoke of, isolate our language
until it means nothing, filling new wings, abstracted, beating
a hurricane, half a world away. Returning to Kierkegaard Ward,
it is magic hour, as sisters draw on Gauloises on the stoop.
The orisha of the doorways is smiling.

Awake is a concept taken for granted
by those who never fear sleep.
Alive is an eternity in realisation that it is vital to stretch
a definition or two, if it means living free.

Stressor: Long Seconds

Here, coming to mind, the *stress* module on my
undergraduate psychology course: how I
thought it would be all about mindfulness
and management, but then how we spent
six months learning how systemic oppression
and structural inequalities can, over enough time,
rewrite internal organs and shorten lives...

Stress hormones (although having adaptive
significance) have no place in this modern society,
because, in its repeating stressful situations,
cortisol, epinephrine and norepinephrine,
the fight or flight mechanisms bubbling within
availability of blood sugar, increasing heart rate,
alertness stimulating synapses and muscle fibres,
increasing respiration, supercharging digestion,
these natural responses are often misread as escalations.

Joy Gardner, 1993

Coming to mind
how no one ever tells you that, when it is your turn,
stress hormones will burn through you like a wildfire,
blinding lights in tunnel vision, hypervigilance
collapsing under its own weight, into an express train
of thought fixating on one-track minutiae,
devilish details like: taser on the left, pistol on the right.
Are they clipped in? Can I reach them when we fight?

No one ever tells you that, flashing before your eyes,
words lose all meaning as time unwinds,
set to spinning by hopes and dreams and memories
overlapping and receding, retreating before the flood.
a tsunami of rushing blood shelling in your ears,
jungle drumming a warning, and all this will be so loud
you will sink into it and drown...

Azelle Rodney and Jean-Charles de Menezes, 2005

Coming to mind
how no one ever tells you that, when it is your turn,
stress hormones will churn up all the bottled demons
of a lifetime, that when you are the star, when it happens,
local aunties will form a protective ring filming
on their phones, circling in salty summoning
(crows at a murder, maybe), mouths shaped O
in the goldfish bowl, where forgetfulness is contagious.
Now, what was I thinking? What did he just say?
What the fuck did I put in my bag today?

No one ever tells you words lose all meaning
as time unwinds, set to spinning, how the urge to struggle free
is hardwired. How so much effort, so much presence of mind
is required to not fight, to not fly,
when so much pressure is applied…

Dalian Atkinson, 2016

Coming to mind
how no one ever tells you that, when it is your turn,
stress hormones will surge, boiling into emotions,
clouds of explosives seeking a spark.
Did taser cop, the young-looking one, just call me son?
Was he even born when Dalian Atkinson scored
that goal of the season, to the soundtrack of 'Life of Riley'
by the Lightning Seeds? Am I allowed to be this angry?
Is it safe for me?

No one ever tells you, in your life flashing before your eyes,
words lose all meaning, as time unwinds in
bubbling blood sugar, heartrate increasing
alertness stimulating respiration, increasing digestion,
supercharging synapses,
everything set to spinning,
and no one ever tells you focusing on your breathing
only helps when you can *breathe*.

It is the first anniversary
of George Floyd being murdered for an alleged
misdemeanour. They blindside me, grab me and pin me,
and, pinched like vice,
I don't know how, and I don't know why,
but, stress hormones raging,
I remember to comply.

Between the Lines (Sewell Report Coupling)

The 'Making of Modern Britain' teaching resource is our response,
Whitewash in different shades, always part of a master's toolbox...

To negative calls for 'decolonising' the curriculum,
We will offer large vats of whitewash, stirring brushes with them.

Neither the banning of white authors
Or our brushes will fail to obscure

Token expressions of Black achievement.
We mix the wash thick, it sets like cement.

Help to broaden young minds
In the way we prescribe.

We have argued against bringing down statues.
Our idols are devils, we know we are too.

We want all children to reclaim their British heritage,
However they gained it, whoever imposed it.

There is a new story about the Caribbean experience,
We made these new cultures, by displacing and uprooting,

Which speaks to the slave period,
That British pride in it remains,

Not only being about profit and suffering,
But also, in how it keeps flags for its summoning.

Symptomatic: Temperatures Run High

On these streets, so easy to believe the etymology
of malevolence is from *male violence*,
even when you know it isn't. Pervasive patriarchy
feeds a need to use strength, to project hypermasculinity
to protect, as it forgets that any arms race
rarely stops with those who cast the biggest shadow…

Here, all words are intimidatory, the voices
that raise them are intimidatory, and the postures
that project them are intimidatory.

It has been learned implicitly, wrapped in gender roles,
accepted with the complicity of silence, even though
the mounting evidence stands before us all, several hands high.
In the ranks now flag-backed, filing in tightly wound
pristine uniformity, wound up to snap, wrapped extensions
of a crown, these thorns of empire, are marching forth to war,
unholy soldiers again, in unison chanting MOVE BACK.

Faces contorted by the ugliness of blind fealty,
seething berserker throwbacks, all atavistic arms, batons
of loyalty and rhythmic beats intimidatory, conducting
the overseer implementation of policy, of the whip hand,
protecting those who own and their property only,
ever drawing new lines in the sand with mission creep and
MOVE BACK.

Their garrisons are again patrolling these colonies
with impunity, revisiting their origins; bad apples
never fall from the poisonous tree. This is not consent.
Male violence never understood consent. MOVE BACK.

And the clock regresses to tics, the calendar retreats centuries,
beating a rhythm, blue centurions are several ranks deep,
sirens screeching white noise, amplified by corrupting power,
drowning out those of us whose turn it is to speak.
Their protection is a racket, too late if you can hear it.

And today we are realising their shields were always weapons,
even before considering how malevolence will use them.

Tsundoku Takotsubo

blossom drifts
fallen tears of spring
mourning snow angels

The window is measuring how well he is coping
by the height of the stack on bedside table. Recently
it has risen to be an honoured kaiju, pages scraping
sky, unopened promises casting long memories,
shadows of a high noon he has not seen clearly
in months. *The buying of more books than one can read
is nothing less than the soul reaching toward infinity.*
There are ghosts here. Outside, the streets echo.

There was a decision taken, by those who saw fit,
to welfare check in rotation. Repetition is a burden.
*It takes three weeks to form a habit, but an instant to lose
perspective.*
Confines are time on the wrists watched. A ronin
has his honour, so they say nothing of it as it passes.
Diligence clearing the detritus of battle, blunted blades,
used mugs, meal trays. His need to escape is real, so
they leave him books. A watchtower kaiju, growing.

The screens are ringing red roses, with everything at issue.
He articulates he misses you. Attentiveness leaving no
loose ends for a tourniquet. He holds the new tome
to his chest, hoping soon to follow you, through
a plothole or narrative misstep. We all fall down.
Words, a murmuration, feathering flesh, swelling
heartfelt into misshapen, inescapable gravity. These tentacles
of cardiomyopathy, somnambulant seppuku, a ronin must travel.

This is a giant in the sandbox, scorpion in the dunes
to spice his nature, invisible hand of industry crescent-
shaped moon drawing lines and gathering tides,
a beachhead, prismatic consciousness, while out walking.
*How do I know what I am thinking, until I have read
the thoughts back in a different place, to the one
that birthed them?* He says, *Never trust a thought that didn't come
by walking,* Baby steps, it all unravels, as he and I become one again.

summer wilderness
rebirth is grief making
hay in emptiness

Matryoshka

That feeling of déjà vu you are having
is your consciousness
being tickled by a quantum supercomputer
running a simulation of this outbreak in the near future

That feeling of déjà vu you are having
is the realisation
that this is the simulation
and that you died years ago

That feeling of déjà vu you are having
is the infinite
symmetries of scale and fractal repetition
of a simulation
                of a simulation
of a simulation
                having this same thought

That feeling of déjà vu you are having is
$n = n + 1$

First Past the Post

crisp common Sunday morning
(well, technically afternoon)
two boys and their father running
approaching from behind
the sun still low
snoozed noontime hazing
and they are chatting as they are jogging
I love how we can never make a decision
the shorter one says
their joy at the inefficiencies
of democracy
free as their feet
staying with me
head bowed
heading home in the tyranny of self

Breakthrough

*Clench a fist
and hold it
to your chest,*

you say,

*not quite centred,
just off to the left.*

That is the size
and shape of your heart,

you say.

Both grow in proportion with you,

whispers every replay,
missing out the part
where mine is ever a fist clenched,
knowing it will never hold yours again.

If you think you're too small to make a difference, try spending the night with a mosquito.

African proverb

Debris Holding Hands on Shingle

Clichés have their place
on the tip of my tongue,
envious of the bead of sweat
clinging to your neck,
suspended on stolen breath,
a time dilation,
flying spaghettification
of a deep space eye,
swallowing our lifelines.

You say,
Certain words should never be used in poetry, like just.

But I remember that day,
walking arm in arm, a trick of light
in plain sight blended with candied cotton clouds
floating above the Broadwalk.

How we sunk into its crowd
more like us, became gaseous, translucent,
an anonymous slow shutter blur.

How freeing it was to be uniformity for a time,
to be seen as *just* friends, as *just* another couple,
as just anything
                            unremarkable.

Golem

Nachküssen; consciousness is always
moments behind such actions
near-autonomous motion
before the will engages
seemed natural
to wake me

and in your favour, the key to our coexistence
the notion that even heaven respects some
boundaries, while timeless whispers shall
distort the rest, stitched seams
dina d'malkhuta dina
in pieces of me, reassembled found footage
lost stories sunk into rock, an icy mountain top
freeze-frame replays, finger-moulded clay
stolen fire as breath, made shapeshifting
alien in sepia memories, set terracotta
guarding beyond life, beyond death
made flesh in these dreams, your silly putty
where your lips press truth
to my forehead
to wake me

Revolutionaries

Every six days, some place somewhere
is celebrating independence from here

as in our streets the people are being
arrested for dissent, for being frogs
who have dared notice the weather
getting warmer, for being desperate
enough to turn the gas off, to get off
the fence and refuse to pay rent
to the fires still burning.

And you and I are snuggling undercover
as placards become petards, as the rhetoric
spikes and ignites, the sky falls, and we take
a pause to pirouette on a pillow's edge, to turn
to each other and confess, *I threw a brick once.*

For we are old enough to remember
the fall of empire, and a curtain made of iron,
so today, having started something, we lie in,
knowing that there will be time before
the dancing ends. We hold tight with each step,
knowing that if we must dance for our oppressors,
then it should be a slow dance, to the beat
of war drums, to show them the beauty
in our threat, the danger of our love.

Maxwell Smart and the Trick of the Light

Tear film bends in remembering. A twinkle
conjuring a common language of folkloric woods.

And I hear you, on solitary path, from a house to a single room.
Through dappled gunfire, monsters of utility with the faces
of men, bayonet teeth to line the maw. Falling through
mattresses of straw and lice. Scratching things together,
like living.

A boy, wandering, rags on his feet, becomes scavenging archivist,
collating future art therapies, forever improvising from debris,
warm reliquaries of mischief, gathered in upcycled X-ray film
(filched for the plastic), made into artful covers for Magen David.

You make yourself useful, cutting flour to stretch the seasoning
of grief. A student of invisibility, spinning veils from mundane
things, from winter trees whistling with crystallised memory,
gossamer fragile like diaphanous flesh.
Always hungry, but hoping to remain unseen.

I hear you, in our common language, in both at us at twelve;
in overdue stories of lost boys, broken, and in our woods.
In canvases made of ourselves, tricksters of the light, all quick wit
and adaptive defences, to catch refractions and stay in shadow.

I hear you, in the smoke, hiding between spindle limbs
of what might have been. Long-lost dreams of belonging,
now fallen, fading tricksters ever bargaining,
signalling from the time before the flood,
the secrets in our blood whispering...

Nephilim.

And I see myself in him, still twinkling in your eyes,
as you tell defiant stories of the Boy in the Woods, Who Survived.

Molotov

And it has me wondering, where will I be
when the first brick in our city becomes a missile?

When soft bedding becomes a fortification again.
When, in the makeshift bunker, production lines
form into fragile fractals, coalescing around notions
of freedom we shared without speaking.

When rebellion has rendered itself
in effigy, in straw man wicker, in waxwork figurines,
interwoven thermal plastics with wicking fabric bones,
through the volatility of bubbles, in fomented loam,
inhalant iridescences and light dancing
in chemical rainbows, slick on puddles,
and flammable dreams.

When the archivist is remade as alchemist
in the interplay of solvents and solutions,
heady on the lungs.

When thickening agents breathe heavy,
blend and bind with the blood, like Vaseline, sticky
and slippy, insurgent fingers counting magic beans,
spilling from the beanbag split under the weight of us,
and when the sandbox ballast of being too young
to understand this love anchors, but is still a rush.

When alkyl nitrates lighten the head an angel's share,
scented with promise, whispers into burning ears,
a notion of freedom we shared without speaking,

it has me realising what I have become in your hands,
and that when the first brick in our city
becomes a missile, overdue,
wherever I am, I will be there with you.

Every Poet Has a Poem Like This

Fuck the British Empire, Fuck the examples that it set.
Fuck the transatlantic slave trade. Fuck resource theft.
Fuck famine. Especially Fuck famine that is manmade.
Fuck concentration camps, Fuck ethnic cleansing,
Fuck indiscriminate shelling and carpet bombing,
Fuck crusades.

Fuck encircling cities. Fuck divide and rule.
Fuck the idea the people even need ruling.
Fuck guns and bombs and warplanes,
Fuck ever-increasing defence spending,
Fuck armies having fascists in their ranks,
Fuck the police becoming paramilitary
(right down to the correct percentage of fascists in their ranks),
and Fuck tanks.

Fuck wars of conquest. Fuck expansionism.
Fuck spheres of influence and zones of control.
Fuck colonialism.

Fuck proxy wars, Fuck information and cyber wars,
Fuck cold and culture wars,
Fuck war.

Fuck special military operations, Fuck police actions,
Fuck regime change, Fuck making up more palatable names.
It is still Fucking war.

Fuck people fleeing wars becoming refugees.
Fuck running away to not be slaughtered.
Fuck chain-link fences. Fuck barbed wire.
Fuck guard towers and Fuck borders.
Fuck motherlands and fatherlands,
Fuck ethnocentric ideas of order,
And Fuck tanks.

Fuck cruise missiles and drone strikes.
Fuck fly-by-wire murder from a distance,
Fuck autonomous weapon systems,
Fuck DARPA dogs and dancing robots.
Fuck the birth of Skynet.
Fuck drone swarms and facial recognition,
Fuck outdated racial phenotypes underpinning facial recognition,
Fuck the birthplace of this prejudice,
Fuck the ongoing oppression and injustice,
Fuck racism.

Fuck people saying Ukraine is a white people war.
Fuck whataboutisms about brown skin, about Palestine and Yemen.
Fuck that this comparison is even possible
(we have so many wars this comparison is possible).
Fuck war as an answer to anything.
Fuck propaganda, Fuck distraction, Fuck justification,
Fuck redacted documents and waiting fifty years to fill in the blanks,
Fuck war as an answer to anything,
Fuck weapons of mass destruction,
Fuck politicians who won't tell the truth,
Fuck tactical nukes,
Fuck thermobaric weapons and cluster munitions,
Fuck chemical weapons and weapons grown in labs,
and Fuck tanks.

Fuck big swinging dicks,
Fuck their hard man machismo,
Fuck their super-fragile egos,
Fuck flexing muscles and rattling sabres for show,
Fuck big dick energy,
Fuck the fact that we want any of that
in the men we choose to lead.
Fuck toxic masculinity and Fuck the patriarchy
(Fuck the system, I mean),
and, of course, absolutely, positively, Fuck the police.
Fuck police states, Fuck repressive states, Fuck one-party states,
Fuck corruption.

Fuck end stage capitalism.
Fuck all our candidates believing in it.
Fuck billionaires, Fuck oligarchs,
Fuck the fact we don't call our billionaires oligarchs.
Fuck the 1%. Fuck kleptocrats.
Fuck trickle-up economics pushing people to their knees.
Fuck the housing crisis. Fuck the climate crisis.
Fuck the fact the solution to all our crises
is progressive tax but some people won't concede.
Fuck the 1% riding to space while we bleed.

Fuck the fact
we haven't learned to share this world and all its lands,
but most of all, Fuck tanks.

Revision: A Pal in Genesis

Eve will always be: reliquary memories
of the old school library, seeping
upward through creaking boards, porous
walls seething with stretches of racking,
sapping strength, the seemingly endless rows
of white faces staring back accusingly
from the shelves, in the silent judgement
of a jury that were never peers. Appearances
are everything he had been programmed
to believe his saviour would look like.
Her arms, around him, serpentine, whispering.

A finger to the lips is steadying him.
As he feared, he never would recognise himself
in any of the stories held in such regimented spines.
Tantalising imperialism lingering in the zeitgeist,
the rank echoes filing in red lines, he is corrected,
a swinging cat-o'-nine in the tinny-smelling
damp, flavoured with freshly broken black skin. Again
a winnowing, weeping for innocence stolen by rote,
disciplined by myriad chiding voices, by the endless
white faces staring back at him from the stretches
of racking, leaving him believing his saviour
would sound like vices, cartilage creaking, choral
divine alms, through windows stained to blacken
the blue. A burden, refrained tight in leaden framing device,
and the only fantasy he could ever be: the house boy.

Later that summer, it is high afternoon
as a note in Mr Jefferson's history class
unfolds before him, a starlight omen, *Master's tools
will never dismantle master's house...*

A winged seed upon changing winds, from the world tree
outside, landing, dilating with his life, growing sinews,
rooting his limbs, making time his plaything, making fresh
pages from fig leaves and green shoots of possibility.
Reliquary memories: an apple shared. A tale to sell.

The Bends

Last night in Krakow, you dared me
to come with you, bent me double
with a phrase around a pointed finger,
When are we ever going to be this close again?
when I folded as easily as the flyer into your pocket.

At dawn, we splinter from the main party,
still sleeping. Pack ourselves neatly
onto a minibus. On the drive,
you teach me the word *Shoah* as the sun rises.

The air is thick, charged, highly pressurised.
Hard to call this tranquillity beautiful
with the way that it squeezes, colder than it should be.
This place is deeper than the road we have left,
than the far-behind city. You are mouthing a prayer.

We have not been organised enough
to pack food, but hunger is relative,
and the air here is thick, pushing all space-time
out of the gut, rabbit punching, a booted kick
squashing thoughts low, to draw gazes to the ground,
shame compressing lungs into silence, pressing
effervescent nausea, to rustling the trees,
to dissolving into the blood; to remain.
Imagination here is to carry the weight of sky.
The air is thick and hard to breathe.
There are birds here. You sound surprised.

As the sun sets, we return to effusive piazza,
to dancing lights over shimmering cobbles,
to the others, slippery in early evening.
We face their interrogations, still decompressing,
unaccustomed to light, struggling to respond to anything,
even the questions we clearly have answers to, like
Who visits Auschwitz on a stag do?

Dawn has long shadows, like sunset.
I feared then that we had come up too quickly. I still do.

For When They Come Again

As a boy, I once ran so hard   from my queer shadow
that I raced   into the arms of a monster.
A predator's grooming   can look a lot like tutoring,
salt pilloried in reminiscence,   tears away from pages,
extracts silenced like Eurydice,   disappearing into folds of self,
swallowed by pink underworld,   fleshy denuder triangle,
an erasure in this side,   burning bright,
the books   at *Institut für Sexualwissenschaft*,
feelings   to be put to death for.

At the intersection,
a one-man diversity hire   meant as a joke
becomes a joke,   an infographic explaining oppression,
a creeping normalisation,   scrawled graffiti, wedge issues
forming slippery slopes.   They are using slick words
like *eugenics* and *genocide*   in public discourse,
rose-tinted with utility,   selling tyranny
enough to make it palatable.   Outside is cold.

My love is forever taking   more risks than advisable,
taking sides,   to be out in the open
is vulnerable,   today, the vulnerable are to be labelled again,
herded away again,   ringfenced and imprisoned.

At the intersection,   there is a devil teaching
the skills of haunting,   how to be remembered
when hidden away,   when deemed unworthy,
there is artistry   in ghetto economics,
in the soul of survival.

As a boy, I once ran   into the shadows,
learning to be invisible,   shielding as deep cover,
between sheets of paper,   sharpening the gaze
to recognise monsters.

Years ago, they burned the books that held my answers,
but at the crossroads, I shall read them anyway.

Mimesis

Camouflage has two primary purposes in nature:
to avoid predation, and to lie in wait, an ambush hunter...

And we remain top of our food chain, an apex predator,
for those of us disguising primarily do so to hide
from one another, or from someone in particular.

At a formative age, one of our earliest games, hide and go seek,
again and again. *Close your eyes, count to a hundred...*

Prey they never see you, this game never ends,
in matching uniforms, matching intonations and prosody,
masking tell-tale traits, sincerest forms of flattery,

until we crouch together, around the next corner
behind the bricked wall, the tall privet hedge,
hearts racing and out of breath.
Prey they never see you, this game never ends,
like every poem is a little bit sex, a little bit death.

Blurring our edges, finding safety in numbers,
again and again. *Close your eyes, count to a hundred...*

Earning the Title Diva

June 2016

Chess timer chastising his strategy, hanging
boardroom clock louder than memory, facial tics.
He had asked for five minutes, when she had them,
but tensions tied had stolen his tongue for two. Blank.

Floodgates: gambit onslaught, the explanation to HR,
briefing reasons for the meeting. A cortisol taster, wafer
and wine anxiety. How he had bonded with a writer
from Florida over 'America is a Gun' by Brian Bilston.
How, although Florida is a big state, when he had tried to raise
the writer, his message went unread. How this worry was eating
him. He said he did not need to be at home, had to stay
busy. But it might be necessary for allowances to be made,
later, if the situation changed. He stopped for breath. This is the edge,
he said, and I am on it. A ledge with no one to talk us down.

My hypervigilance had been activated at some point
of no return on the District Line that morning, shaken up
by rocking motions, the lullaby wheels recalling the feel
of rumbling bass through my feet. I was back on Frith Street
on May Day bank holiday weekend in '99, a Friday.
Turning right onto Old Compton. Meeting clouds in the west,
this five minutes of programming in endless repeats of
Mr Angry. This morning's tube rhythms fading into
the stampede, as brakes made screams, until again
I could taste masonry dust. Asking who knows first aid. Debris
learning triage in the field. It is not 9am, and I need a whisky.

And I am watching him omit this part of our explanation
to HR, saying merely he cannot trust me to remain stoic
in the office today. Especially in the face of its typical
hypermasculine heteronormativity, with epithets like confetti.
Especially in the wake of what just happened a world away.
How they are too threatening in this new frame. Too
threatening today. I used to do drag, he says. These were my people.
By implication, HR and the rest of the team are not.

Back from the Admiral Duncan, tears are salting the dust;
in our rushing blood, the boardroom clock is lost, as we
resynchronise brainwaves to present. Together again,
'America is a Gun', we say, *You should read it. It might help explain.*
Later, the MD will call us *diva* for the first time, claim
the events are unconnected. We stayed all day. Pride is protest.

Behind the Curtain

> *'You have some queer friends, Dorothy,' she said.*
> *'The queerness doesn't matter, so long as they're friends,'*
> *was the answer.*
> L Frank Baum, *The Road to Oz*

He agrees *we have all been lost boys*, gathering
in stoned circles, fae but called *fairies*,
profound foundlings for applause. Ageless
vogue strobes between, bass making wisps
of words, bubble brain pitch of munchkin
gilded lollipops, skilled lips, sweetened tips
of tongues, sticky salsas of blood sugar, salted
piquant with a DJ's euphoric fizz. It is body
to body language. House drops. Chemicals
grip two-handed, swaying sulphur and nicotine
hips, slinky and addictive. The rainbow
is a promise, and on it, a soft Weegie
dulcet baritone. Ageless, this road of yellow brick,
lions and otters and bears, oh my!

In public, we swathe in honorifics, we codeswitch,
to *mind the gap* receptive. Careful to navigate
the *tally-ho* sassenachs in the centre of the space
without drawing attention. No *ducks*. No *darlings*.
No *babes*. This is kitsune tricksy, shapeshifting
invitational phonemes and postures until gazes
are averted. On this path, in the woods, survival
is becoming a trick of the light. Camouflage
is learning stillness, and how to drown
out that internal critic, monologuing an
expositional punditry of your journey,
Well, lad, you're out, but are you OUT out?

In the chillout, a chattering hivemind, buzzing
with belonging, where all the fur of its glamour
is never the illusion. A fae enchanted garden fixed
forever at magic hour. Our golden pride of lions,
full of courage and cute accents, flattery softening focus,
there is no place like home.
Outside, we find refuge, with the rouge and red light
tales, airbrushing the larks from the dawn.

Later, we will be slipping on spilled rubies in the gutter,
playing mindless straw man games with the universe,
but for now, we are clicking together and wishing.

Traditions in the Hiss of Analogue

Gathering dust, a quintessence is this tome.
Reason enough to turn pages into dreams
Of infinite quantum universes foretold,
Where the weight of us, all our future selves, behold

Angels' spiral, groove on a pinhead as singing valleys,
Gathering dust: a quintessence. Is this tome
Evermore realistic, in scratch and groan,
Liminal in ethereal, in its frequency
Of infinite quantum universes foretold,
Now it's rendered flesh, in dashiki and cast bones?
Ghosts written into the code, inside the machine

Gathering. Dust; a quintessence is. This tome
Record, playing long-dead voices, these skipping stones,
In the still of time, making ripples, scaled symmetry
Of infinite quantum universes foretold.
Tomorrow, they say, Dad will give you stories to hold.

Ever was it so that we kept our history,
Gathering dust; a quintessence is this tome
Of infinite quantum universes foretold.

No one ever wants the job, you see, not really.
It ties you into dreams, with a half-lived life,
Grandma Evelyn warned, as she passed it on to me.
Here where all things are possible, in space between –

It is vital that you remember you carry light.
No one ever wants the job, you see, not really,
Spirits falling to empire so much of this scene.
It is hard to not to lose yourself entirely,
Grandma Evelyn warned, as she passed it on to me.
Here, in the spaces between, in the margins, we breathe.
To bear our standards means many hills on which to die.

No one ever wants the job, you see, not really.
Infinite quantum universes you carry,
Gathering dust, to coalesce the very stuff of life,
Grandma Evelyn warned, as she passed it on to me;
Living this role takes sacrifice, and humility.
It is her voice I still hear in the white noise, not mine.
No one ever wants the job, you see, not really,
Grandma Evelyn warned, as she passed.

Appendix: Once Removed

I once heard it said
infighting in poetry is like two drunks fighting over a telephone box

And in recovery   as my fleshed-out surgeon discusses proudly
how skill can make most traumas imperceptible over time
if the stitches are just right   invisible to the eye
    to all but the brightest in the land
how a practised hand can be redemption
there, editorial spin in the evidence he is presenting
my photographer's mind   sees its beauty
my anthropologist's eye   knows why
as the small boy in me defiantly points his finger
    recognising hubris by its signs

And once upon an anaesthetic
I am recounting backwards   a story
in sigh-metered high-pitched frequencies
bouncing off pristine surfaces of hospitality
finding excruciating resonance
    in their mustering
in a clichéd crowded neon hallway
it is the morning before my surgery
and a testimony has threaded me
    tautly into resuscitated recitation
to a firebrand from Galway   full of notions
she patiently abides by   *nil by mouth*
takes observations as she humours me
    gutted by a katana
she repeats
it is the morning of my surgery

For I once met a man
who had several hundred sutures in a torso patina
    all over the use of a telephone box
he couldn't wait his turn
nor the ninja neither
their addicts' logic, rendering queues moot

whetted reds like palate blades
amuse-bouche   with a snicker-snack
the tale of these skin-caught train tracks
left me with no doubts
a photographer's eye   had shuttered this in preservation
an anthropologist's mind   had unpicked its roots
to cause and aftereffect bifurcations
confections to train the senses
to be recalled
whenever waiting to be fed

As Sensei Kerouac once said
Don't use the phone. People are never ready to answer it. Use poetry

Years later, dreams of it all are still putting me to sleep
because for some of us   happily ever after
is having anyone answer
even if that means being   *gutted by a katana*

Notes

Contraband

Prince Philip, the Duke of Edinburgh, infamously referred to the wiring in a fuse junction box as looking 'as if it was put in by an Indian'.

Atlas Learning Masters' Tools

Hans Eysenck and his theories on IQ and race, now largely debunked, underpinned intelligence testing for decades.

nolite te bastardes carborundorum: 'Don't let the bastards grind you down', as in *The Handmaid's Tale* by Margaret Atwood.

Vitae summa brevis spem nos vetat incohare longam: 'The brief sum of life forbids us the hope of enduring long' – Horace.

quos deus vult perdere prius dementat: 'Those whom the gods would destroy they first make mad'.

Blind Study: Test Subject

First published in *Hair-Raising* by Nine Pens Press (2021).

Canute at the Edge of the World

Written from notes taken in Terrigal on the Central Coast, eastern Australia.

The Skillion is a rock formation in Terrigal.

Wittgenstein's Beetle is a thought experiment on communication and perception.

John Rawls's Veil of Ignorance is a thought experiment on social justice and human inclination to fairness.

Ralph Waldo Emerson's Transparent Eyeball is a thought experiment about being one with the environment and nature, about being absorbing and present rather than biased and editorial.

Corner

There is a legend that blues man Robert Johnson sold his soul to the devil at a crossroads for blues virtuosity…

Office Politics: The Little Boy and The Fat Man

Little Boy and Fat Man were the nuclear bombs dropped on Hiroshima and Nagasaki in 1945.

COP2*: T*sk T*sk

The Blind Men and the Elephant is an eastern parable about the limitations of narrow points of view.

No nation has completed its development, because no advanced nation is yet sustainable: Sir David Attenborough, COP26.

Ode to Elegua: Constitutional Written

Elegua is an orisha, a deity of West African roots. Master of the roads and doorways, he manifests as both an old man and a little boy.

Anxiety is the dizziness of freedom … Not a problem to be solved, but a reality to be experienced: Søren Kierkegaard.

Between the Lines (Sewell Report Coupling)

Commission on Race and Ethnic Disparities, the Sewell Report 2021 was commissioned by Boris Johnson's Conservative government in response to the Black Lives Matter movement resurgence following the death of George Floyd in May 2020. The lines in italics are direct quotes from this report.

Symptomatic: Temperatures Run High

Written in response to seeing riot police striking sitting protestors with their shields in order to 'disperse' them.

Tsundoko Takotsubo

First published in *Untitled Voices*, issue 4 (Untitled, 2022).

Tsundoko: the pile of unread books left, typically, on a bedside table.

Takotsubo cardiomyopathy: the technical name for 'broken heart syndrome', when grief causes a cardiac event.

Kaiju: giant monster in Japanese culture; think Godzilla and Mothra.

Seppuku: ritual suicide committed by samurai

Debris Holding Hands on Shingle

The Broadwalk is in Brighton, West Sussex.

Golem

Nachküssen: German word for a kiss that makes up for all the kisses that have been missed due to absence, forgotten or overlooked.

dina d'malkhuta dina: Hebrew, rabbinic teaching 'the law of the land is the law', meaning that the civil law of the country is binding upon Jewish inhabitants of said country. Corollary of 'Render unto Caesar that which is Caesar's'.

Revolutionaries

Every six days, some place somewhere/is celebrating independence from here: reference to the most celebrated national holiday on Earth being independence from Britain day. The average frequency is in fact seven days, but six worked better with the Eden subtext. ;)

Maxwell Smart and the Trick of the Light

From a Poetry School course with Anna Veprinska. We wrote after the testimony of a Holocaust survivor; mine was Maxwell Smart, born 1 June 1930 in Buczacz, Poland (now Ukraine). Having escaped the liquidation of the ghetto he went into the forest alone as a child, where he hid and managed to survive with only occasional help until liberation. I simply do not understand how this man is not a household name, so here is my humble attempt to help this.

For When They Come Again

Institut für Sexualwissenschaft (1919–1933) was a private sexology clinic in Germany which was targeted and destroyed by the Nazis. Those burning books… There is reason queer identity seems like a 'new thing'.

Robert Johnson again.

Earning the Title Diva

Published as a spoken word piece by Nymphs & Thugs in 2021 as part of a memorial project marking the fifth anniversary of the Pulse nightclub shooting (*Sometimes, the Revolution Is Small*, Nymphs & Thugs, 2021).

Neo-Nazi David Copeland, the bomber of the Admiral Duncan in May 1999, called himself Mr Angry.

Traditions in the Hiss of Analogue

First published in *Untitled Voices*, issue 3 (Untitled, 2021).

Appendix: Once Removed

First published in Untitled Voices, issue 3 (Untitled, 2021).

Don't use the phone. People are never ready to answer it. Use poetry: Jack Kerouac.

Acknowledgements

I started my journey with poetry as a teenager, and then stopped for about fifteen years after giving in to the pervasive received wisdom that poetry wasn't for the likes of me. I finally circled back at thirty-seven, and fell into the arms of the most welcoming scene one could ever wish to find. First to be thanked have to be those brilliant poets in London full of passion and vision that gave me my fire back. Thank you to the wonderful humans that made Boomerang Club, Chocolate Poetry Club, Genesis Slam, Incite! and Spoken Word London so much like home.

Thanks to all the promoters and organisers that booked me through 2021 and 2022, while this book was being written, and all the audiences who heard the occasional rough cut of some of the poems that I have included. With special mention to Rebecca Tantony for the set at the Phantom Laundry at Shambala Festival (feeling like a rockstar for a day was a trip).

Thanks to Ollie and Nicola of Untitled Voices, and Matt of Nymphs & Thugs, and the various anthologies in which a few of these poems were first published.

Thanks to Andrew McMillan, Stephen Sexton, and Cynthia Miller and the Arvon Foundation for your wonderful workshops that inspired many of the pieces here (and beyond).

Special thanks to Anna Veprinska and the Poetry School for the invaluable course on *Writing the Holocaust* that introduced me to the story of Maxwell Smart and gave me the courage and helped me find a voice to retell his story in some small part.

And, of course, massive thanks to Arts Council England for the award of the Develop Your Creative Practice grant that gave me the resources to invest in myself and attend the aforementioned workshops.

Thanks to Apples and Snakes and the Red Sky Sessions series for becoming a vital accountability buddy that ensured that I kept writing in the more isolating times during the pandemic.

Thanks to Dr Lee Campbell, Hannah Chutzpah, Rebecca Cooney, Peter DeGraft-Johnson, Kayla Feldman, Kat Francois, Nikita Gill, Salena Godden, Jem Henderson, Jonathan Kinsman, Tyrone Lewis, James McDermott, Barbara O'Donnell, George Parker, Fay Roberts, Roger Robinson, Myriam San Marco, JP Seabright, Dan Simpson, Yomi Sode, Joelle Taylor and Jake Wild-Hall for being simultaneously amazing supporters and perpetual inspirations.

And finally, massive thanks to Clive and Bridget at Burning Eye, and the brilliant editing of Harriet Evans, for making all this possible and continuing to have faith in whatever it is I am trying to do.

Excelsior!